DESTINATION
URANUS, NEPTUNE, AND PLUTO

GILES SPARROW

PowerKiDS
press

New York

Published in 2010 by The Rosen Publishing Group
29 East 21st Street, New York, NY 10010

U.S. Editor: Kara Murray

Picture Credits
Key: t – top, b – below, c – center, l – left, r – right. iStockphoto: Lars
Lentz 9; NASA: 2-3, 24b, 24-25, ESA 10r, GRIN TP, 15t, 16, 21, JHU 28, JPL
11, 12b, 13, 14, 15b, 20-21, 22b, JSC 6-7; PD-USGOV: 27t; Photos.com:
10l, 27b; Science Photo Library: Chris Butler 29, David A. Hardy 16-17,
NASA 12t, Sheila Terry 26, Detlev Van Ravenswaay 22-23; Shutterstock:
George Toubalis 2, 4, 6, 18, 19

Front cover: NASA: bl, GRIN c; Back cover: GRIN; Backgrounds: NASA

Library of Congress Cataloging-in-Publication Data

Sparrow, Giles.
  Destination Uranus, Neptune, and Pluto / Giles Sparrow.
      p. cm. — (Destination solar system)
  Includes index.
  ISBN 978-1-4358-3446-0 (lib. bdg.) — ISBN 978-1-4358-3463-7 (pbk.) —
ISBN 978-1-4358-3464-4 (6-pack)
  1. Uranus (Planet)—Juvenile literature. 2. Neptune (Planet)—Juvenile
literature. 3. Pluto (Dwarf planet)—Juvenile literature. I. Title.
  QB681.S628 2010
  523.47—dc22
                                        2009002985

Manufactured in China

CONTENTS

>>>>>>> >>>>>>>

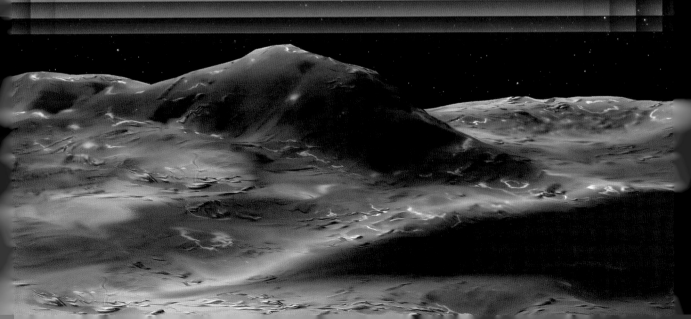

WHERE ARE THE OUTER PLANETS?

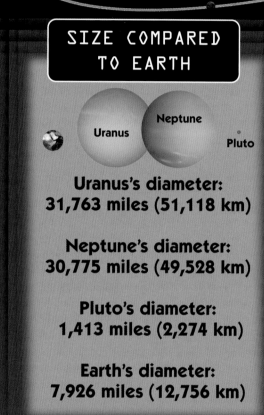

Uranus and Neptune are the most distant of the planets. Farther out still is Pluto, the best known of the dwarf planets.

Uranus, Neptune, and Pluto are trapped by the Sun's powerful **gravity** and travel around the Sun along paths, called **orbits**. Their orbits are far out in space, where the Sun is little more than a bright star.

Uranus is your first stop. It is 19 times farther out than Earth and takes much longer to orbit the Sun. Uranus's year—the time it takes to orbit the Sun once—lasts 84 Earth years. Neptune is even farther away, orbiting the Sun once every 164 Earth years at a distance of 2.8 **billion** miles (4.5 billion km).

SIZE COMPARED TO EARTH

Uranus

Neptune

Pluto

Uranus's diameter:
31,763 miles (51,118 km)

Neptune's diameter:
30,775 miles (49,528 km)

Pluto's diameter:
1,413 miles (2,274 km)

Earth's diameter:
7,926 miles (12,756 km)

DISTANCE FROM THE SUN

This diagram shows how far away the outer planets are. Neptune and Pluto are too far to see with the naked eye, but Uranus is just visible if you know where to look.

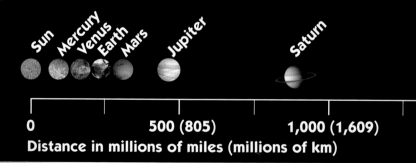

Sun Mercury Venus Earth Mars Jupiter Saturn

| 0 | 500 (805) | 1,000 (1,609) |

Distance in millions of miles (millions of km)

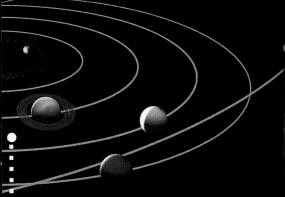

The solar system is made up of the Sun, the planets, and the asteroid belt—a ring of rocks that orbit between Mars and Jupiter.

Uranus and Neptune are like twins. They are both **ice giants**—balls of slushy ice— and are similar sizes. Each one could swallow up 50 Earths!

Pluto is a dwarf planet. It is only about two-thirds as wide as Earth's Moon. It orbits beyond the eight main planets most of the time. Sometimes its odd-shaped orbit comes in closer than Neptune's. Pluto's year is longer than any planet, taking a staggering 248 Earth years to complete just one orbit around the Sun.

Getting to Uranus

The time it takes to get to Uranus depends on how you travel. These figures suppose you travel in a straight line at a constant speed, but in reality it would take longer.

Distance from Earth to Uranus
Closest   1.7 billion miles
             (2.7 billion km)
Farthest   1.9 billion miles
             (3 billion km)

By car at 70 miles per hour (113 km/h)
Closest   2,770 years
Farthest   3,100 years

By rocket at 7 miles per second (11 km/s)
Closest   7 years, 8 months
Farthest   8 years, 7 months

Time for radio signals to reach Uranus (at the speed of light)
Closest   2 hours, 32 minutes
Farthest   2 hours, 47 minutes

Uranus

Neptune

Pluto

| 2,000 (3,219) | 2,500 (4,023) | 3,000 (4,828) | 3,500 (5,633) |

THE FLIGHT TO
URANUS

Imagine you are going on a **mission** to the outer planets. The journey will take a whole lifetime. For much of the time, you will be asleep in **suspended animation** so you do not grow too old on the long flight.

LOOKING FROM EARTH

Before setting off, you decide to look at the planets from Earth. Only Uranus, the closest and brightest of the three, is visible without a telescope. Even that is just a faint point of light. Neptune and Pluto can be seen only with a telescope. Through the most powerful telescopes, Uranus is green and Neptune is blue, but Pluto still looks like a dim smudge.

LONG FLIGHT

Your giant spaceship starts slowly but its engine will fire for years, steadily getting you to a high speed. Even once you are whizzing through space, the journey to Uranus will take 15 years.

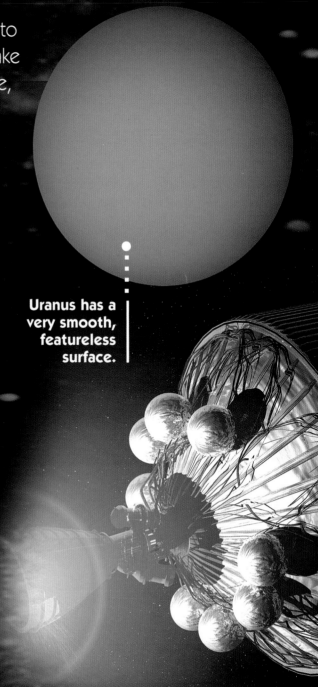

Uranus has a very smooth, featureless surface.

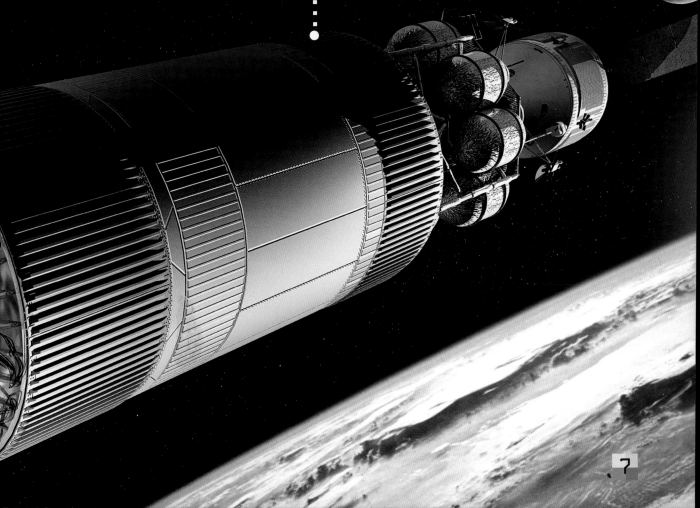

ON ITS SIDE

Like all planets, Uranus is spinning. However, you notice something strange about it. Uranus is tipped over, with one of the poles facing the Sun. As a result, the planet rolls along as it orbits the Sun, instead of spinning like a top as other planets do.

CALM PLANET

As you approach Uranus, you are woken by the ship's computers. A huge green planet is straight ahead. It looks pale because sunlight is very weak this far out.

Uranus looks as smooth as an egg. Unlike the gas giants, Jupiter and Saturn, Uranus's green **atmosphere** has no signs of storms or windy weather. Beneath the calm atmosphere, Uranus is probably a slushy liquid and ice.

Your spacecraft is too heavy to be sent off from the surface of Earth. Instead, it has been constructed in the weightlessness of space.

IN ORBIT

Your spaceship goes into orbit above the green planet. Even this close, there is little to see in the atmosphere.

FAINT RINGS

The almost featureless planet below is a letdown. However, you noticed the sunlight **flickering** as you went into orbit. You know what that means, Uranus must have **rings**. You cannot see them, so they must be very thin and faint. Your spacecraft's **radar** soon finds them for you. The rings are only 3 feet (1 m) wide and made up of billions of chunks of frozen **methane**.

INVISIBLE WINDS

You turn the radar onto the planet below. You realize that even though it looks calm, there is a lot happening in the atmosphere. Strong winds are blowing around the planet at up to 360 miles per hour (580 km/h). The air **temperature** is −350 °F (−212 °C).

Uranus's axis is almost horizontal. Earth's is nearly vertical. As a result, Uranus spins at a right angle to the direction of its orbit.

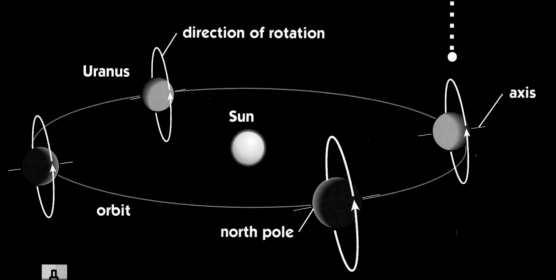

direction of rotation

Uranus

Sun

axis

orbit

north pole

TILTED FIELD

A sensor detects Uranus's **magnetic field**, which **rotates** along with the planet. It turns out that Uranus is rotating once every 17 hours.

On most planets, the **magnetic poles** are close to the north **pole** and south pole. On Uranus, the field is wildly out of line. Even stranger, the magnetic field does not even pass through the center of the planet. What has made Uranus so unusual?

A YEAR AND A DAY

Uranus's tilt gives the planet strange days and years. Uranus's year lasts 84 Earth years. For roughly half of each year, the north pole is in constant sunlight and it is summer in the north. Then winter begins as the north is plunged into night for the next 42 years. The length of days and nights depends on where you are on Uranus. At the poles, the Sun is up for 42 Earth years. Near the equator, the Sun rises and sets every eight hours!

Uranus's rings are much fainter than Saturn's. The rings also circle over the top of the planet, not around the side.

URANUS'S MOONS

Ariel shows up as a bright spot against the surface of Uranus. The moon is also casting a shadow on the planet.

Before setting off for Neptune, you decide to take a quick tour of Uranus's large family of 18 moons.

WHAT'S IN A NAME?

The moons of Uranus are named after characters from English literature. All but two of them come from plays by William Shakespeare. Miranda and Ariel (right) are from *The Tempest*. Titania and Oberon are fairies from *A Midsummer Night's Dream*.

MAJOR MOONS

Most of Uranus's moons are less than 50 miles (80 km) wide, little more than giant icy rocks. However, five are much larger. These are known as the major moons. In order from Uranus, they are Miranda, Ariel, Umbriel, Titania, and Oberon. Ariel and Umbriel are both around 730 miles (1,170 km) across. Titania and Oberon are the largest, about 960 miles (1,550 km) wide, or half the width of Earth's Moon. All the major moons aremade from a mixture of rock, ice, and frozen methane.

BROKEN SURFACE

First up is Miranda, the smallest of the major moons at 300 miles (480 km) wide. This moon turns out to be one of the weirdest worlds in the **solar system**. Miranda's surface is a crazy patchwork of different landscapes that do not match each other. It is as if the moon was broken apart and put back together messily. Perhaps you will find more clues to this mystery by visiting Uranus's other moons.

CRACKING UP

As you fly past, you can see Ariel is covered in deep canyons that divide the surface up into chunks. The bottoms of these canyons are flat, perhaps they were once flooded with slushy ice that froze completely solid.

Next you arrive at Umbriel. This battered world is covered with millions of **impact craters**. That suggests that Umbriel's surface is very old.

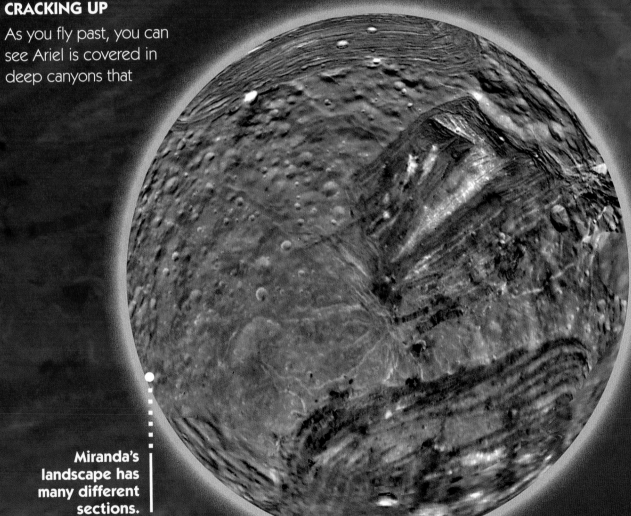

Miranda's landscape has many different sections.

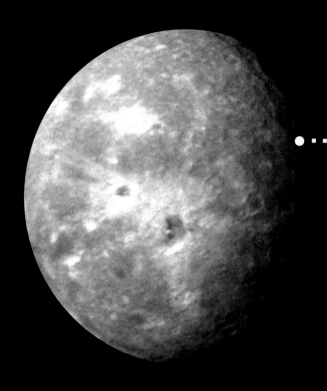

Some of Oberon's large craters are surrounded by rays of pale ice that sprayed out after the moon was hit by large space rocks.

like their larger and hotter neighbors. Where does the heat come from to power these changes?

Astronomers think that Miranda and Ariel are stretched and squeezed by by gravity from Uranus and from the outer moons. This warms the moons in a process called **tidal heating**. Tidal heating explains Miranda's broken surface. The heat melted the moon's **crust** so large chunks of it sunk into the **mantle** underneath!

HOT INSIDE

Farther out from Uranus, you pass Titania and Oberon. These moons are less cratered than Umbriel. Both also have canyons like those on Ariel.

Large moons hold more heat inside them, which can cause **volcanoes** and **geysers** to erupt onto the surface and cover craters. Titania and Oberon are the largest moons, so their craters are regularly covered by eruptions —more so than on smaller Umbriel. That is why Umbriel looks so cratered.

PUSHED AND PULLED

Ariel and Miranda are even smaller than Umbriel, but their surfaces still look like they have been cracking and shifting

The canyons on Ariel were created when the moon became hot and swelled. As it cooled, the icy crust cracked.

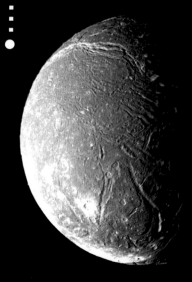

HEADING FOR
NEPTUNE

The journey to Neptune takes another ten years. You wake from suspended animation to find the spaceship in orbit. Neptune appears out of the gloom as a dimly lit blue globe.

BLUE GIANT

Neptune is almost the same size as Uranus but there are some clear differences. Neptune's weather looks very violent. The planet has many dark and light cloud bands that remind you of the stripes on Jupiter and Saturn. And you can see right away that Neptune is not tilted over like Uranus.

The most striking feature on Neptune is a large dark spot near the **equator**. This is a giant storm, similar to Jupiter's Great Red Spot.

COLD CONDITIONS

Although Neptune receives much less heat from the Sun than Uranus does, its upper atmosphere is about the same temperature, at –350 °F (–212 °C).

Neptune is named for the Roman god of the sea. The planet's dark blue color reminded astronomers of the ocean.

The time between sunrise and sunset on Neptune is just 16 hours. This shows that Neptune spins much faster than Earth.

WINDY WORLD

As you get close to the planet, you measure the wind speed in the upper atmosphere. The wind turns out to be 1,250 miles per hour (2,000 km/h). That makes Neptune the windiest place in the solar system! The winds seem to get faster higher up. The fastest-moving clouds on the planet are small white clouds called scooters that circle Neptune in 78 hours.

MAGNETIC SHIFT

Like on Uranus, Neptune's magnetic field is tilted away from the poles. If Earth's magnetic field were tilted as much, our planet's north magnetic pole would be as far away from the North Pole as Chicago.

Getting to Neptune

The time it takes to reach Neptune depends on how you travel. These figures suppose you travel in a straight line at a constant speed, but in reality it would take longer.

Distance from Earth to Neptune
Closest	2.7 billion miles (4.3 billion km)
Farthest	2.9 billion miles (4.7 billion km)

By car at 70 miles per hour (113 km/h)
Closest	4,400 years
Farthest	4,730 years

By rocket at 7 miles per second (11 km/s)
Closest	12 years, 3 months
Farthest	13 years, 2 months

Time for radio signals to reach Neptune (at the speed of light)
Closest	4 hours, 8 minutes
Farthest	4 hours, 12 minutes

MOONS AND RINGS

MOONS AND RINGS

Neptune

Neptune's moons are tiny compared to their parent planet. Even the largest one, Triton, is dwarfed by Neptune.

Triton

The weather conditions are too dangerous to fly into Neptune's atmosphere, so you turn your attention to the planet's **satellites**.

LUMPS OF ICE

Neptune has eight main moons. As you fly toward them, you glide over a set of strange rings. They are much thicker on one side of the planet than the other.

Neptune's five small inner moons are chunks of rock and ice. The largest is just 65 miles (105 km) wide. They are shepherd moons, so named because they "herd" Neptune's rings into circles.

BIG THREE

Next are Neptune's three largest moons: Proteus, Triton, and Nereid.

You get only a glimpse of dark Proteus and Nereid as you head for Triton. Triton is slightly smaller than Earth's Moon and orbits Neptune in the opposite direction from all the other moons.

Neptune's rings are very faint. Some parts are broken into arcs.

The moon Triton has fewer craters than its neighbors. The surface must have been covered in fresh ice recently.

BRIGHT ICE

The closer you get to Triton, the more this moon seems out of place. It is much brighter than the others. It also has an atmosphere of mainly nitrogen. This is also the most common gas in Earth's air, but Triton has no **oxygen** at all.

As you begin your approach for landing, you see that Triton's icy surface looks cracked. There are also mysterious dark streaks of soot.

COLD VOLCANOES

The ground is rock-solid ice. The temperature is –391 °F (–235 °C), making Triton the coldest-known place in the solar system. Your landing site was once a river of slush but has now frozen solid. Astronomers think Triton's icy inside is heated by the pull of Neptune's gravity. This heating produces volcanoes that erupt slush instead of **lava**.

TRITON'S SEASONS

Triton's orbit combines with Neptune's to give the moon a 688-year cycle of seasons. Each pole receives hundreds of years of sunlight during its summer, followed by hundreds of years of freezing darkness in winter. During winter, the thin air freezes on the ground and changes the color of Triton's surface. In summer, the frozen air evaporates, blows around Triton as a gentle wind, and freezes again at the other pole. Some frozen air gets trapped underground and produces pockets of gas as it warms up. These burst out of the ground as geysers, throwing black dust into the air as they erupt.

DUST FOUNTAIN

Suddenly the ground starts trembling and you fall over. Seconds later, a fountain of black dust and gas bursts out of a crack in the ground. It is a geyser. The geyser reaches a spectacular height in the low gravity, before blowing sideways in a gentle wind. Sooty dust grains begin to fall back to the ground, producing one of the dark streaks across the landscape you saw from space.

Triton's geysers send jets of gas many miles (km) into the sky.

17

INSIDE URANUS AND NEPTUNE

As you prepare to move on to Pluto, you puzzle over why Uranus and Neptune can be so similar in some ways but very different in others.

HEAT SOURCE

Why is Uranus so calm while Neptune is so windy? And why is Neptune the same temperature as Uranus when it is so much farther from the Sun? The only explanation is that Neptune has a source of heat inside it. Your spaceship's sensors reveal that the planet is pumping out twice as much heat as it receives from the Sun.

GAS LAYER

Uranus and Neptune look similar inside. The outer atmospheres are made mostly of the lightweight gases **hydrogen** and **helium**. There is also a small amount of methane, which gives the planets their bluish green color. Neptune's

Uranus consists mostly of layers of gas, liquid, and ice that merge together with no definite boundaries. In the center of the planet is a core of solid rock.

ocean

ice

rock core

atmosphere has slightly more methane than its neighbor, so it appears bluer.

WARM ICE

Deeper inside Neptune, the gases gradually turn to liquid as **pressure** pushes down on them. Roughly a quarter of the way in, the liquid layer gives way to a layer of slushy ice made of water, ammonia, and other heavy chemicals that have frozen and sunk toward the center of the planet.

This ice layer takes up most of each planet's volume. That is why the planets are sometimes referred to as ice giants. The ice is squeezed tightly by gravity and it is very hot and half melted. Currents in the hot slush swirl the inside of the planet around, creating a magnetic field.

HARD CENTER

At the center of both Neptune and Uranus is a solid **core** of rock that has most of each planet's **mass**. Uranus's core is about the size of Earth, Neptune's is probably larger.

HOT STUFF

Astronomers think the middle of Neptune is getting smaller under its own gravity and producing heat as the pressure rises. Jupiter and Saturn do this, too. Uranus is the only giant planet that does not give off heat. That is why its weather is so calm.

ocean

hot, slushy ice

rock core

Neptune's inside is thought to be similar to Uranus's, but its core is larger and hotter.

HOW THE ICE GIANTS FORMED

Uranus and Neptune both formed shortly after the Sun began to shine, roughly 4.5 billion years ago. The young Sun was surrounded by a vast cloud of gas and dust that became the planets.

OUTER CLOUD

The planets of the inner solar system are small and solid because the inner part of the cloud had mostly rock and metal in it. The outer part was rich in water and gases, which had been blown out of the inner solar system by the Sun's energy. The giant planets—Jupiter, Saturn, Uranus, and Neptune—formed largely from these materials.

DUST AND ICE

Uranus and Neptune probably formed from the core outward. As dust particles in the cloud collided and stuck together, they grew gradually into **planetesimals** —balls of rock with enough gravity to pull more material onto them. As the planetesimals grew even bigger, they began to pull in gases from the cloud and form thick atmospheres.

The ice giants formed from the cold outer region of a cloud that surrounded the young Sun.

Icy Triton formed in a different part of the solar system than Neptune.

Uranus and Neptune are smaller than the gas giants, Jupiter and Saturn, because they formed where the cloud of gas and dust was thinnest.

BANGS AND CRASHES

The early history of the solar system was violent. The young planets were often struck by smaller planetesimals, **comets**, and **asteroids**. One especially violent collision probably caused Uranus's unusual tilt by knocking the planet on its side. This probably happened long ago because Uranus's moons have since settled back into stable orbits. Some astronomers think the collision that knocked Uranus over might have let out all the planet's internal heat.

WHERE DID TRITON COME FROM?

Astronomers think that Triton used to be a planet, with its own orbit around the Sun. Then a large collision sent Triton hurtling toward Neptune. Neptune's strong gravity caught Triton and trapped it in a backward orbit. Triton itself then pulled on several of Neptune's other moons, absorbing them or shooting them away from the Neptune system.

NEXT STOP
PLUTO

The journey to Pluto, the dwarf planet, takes another 20 years. It looks tiny after the giant worlds you have visited before.

Pluto is more colorful than Charon because chemicals in its atmosphere freeze on the surface.

CROSSING PATHS

Pluto's orbit crosses Neptune's, meaning it is sometimes closer to the Sun than the blue ice giant. However, the stretch and tilt of Pluto's path around the Sun means that the two worlds never come close together.

SMALL WORLD

Your ship's engines have to fire hard to slow you down enough to go into orbit. Pluto's gravity is very weak compared to that of the planets.

Pluto was once said to be the ninth planet and the smallest one by far. It is actually smaller than many of the

Even with the most powerful telescopes, the surface of Pluto is still a blur from Earth.

solar system's moons, including Earth's. In 2006, it was decided that Pluto was too small to be called a planet. Instead, it was reclassified as a dwarf planet.

HUGE PARTNER

As you get closer, you notice a huge moon rising from behind Pluto. This moon, called Charon, is half the width of Pluto, yet it is very close to Pluto—20 times closer than the Moon is to Earth.

Charon

Getting to Pluto

The time it takes to reach Pluto depends on how you travel. These figures suppose you could travel in a straight line at a constant speed, but in reality it would take longer.

Distance from Earth to Pluto	
Closest	2.7 billion miles (4.3 billion km)
Farthest	4.7 billion miles (7.6 billion km)

By car at 70 miles per hour (113 km/h)	
Closest	4,400 years
Farthest	7,660 years

By rocket at 7 miles per second (11 km/s)	
Closest	12 years, 8 months
Farthest	21 years, 3 months

Time for radio signals to reach Pluto (at the speed of light)	
Closest	4 hours, 7 minutes
Farthest	6 hours, 58 minutes

Your ship's instruments tell you that Pluto and its main moon weigh very little, so they are probably made mostly of ice, mixed with just a little rock. They do not have heavy, metal cores like most of the planets.

Astronomers think Charon formed from a chunk of Pluto that was blasted off in a huge collision. Earth's own Moon may have formed in the same way. Pluto and Charon look a lot like Neptune's moon Triton. Perhaps they all formed in the same place?

ON THE DWARF PLANET

You step out onto Pluto's icy surface. In the weak gravity you weigh only a fraction of your Earth weight. You must wear a heavy suit to keep your feet on the ground!

Nix

DARK DAY

It is daytime at the landing site, but you carry a flashlight because the Sun is just a bright star above Pluto. Daytime is as dark as a moonlit night on Earth. Pluto's surface is −382 °F (−230 °C). It is almost as cold as Triton.

THE KUIPER BELT

Pluto, Charon, and Triton all came from a swarm of icy objects beyond Neptune's orbit. This is the Kuiper Belt. The ice is left over from the cloud that once filled the solar system. When they fall into the inner solar system, the objects turn into comets. In 2005, another dwarf planet was discovered in the Kuiper Belt beyond the orbit of Pluto. It was named Eris (below) and was found to be slightly larger than Pluto. Astronomers believe that they will find several more Pluto-sized dwarf planets.

more than seven times the size of a full moon seen from Earth. Pluto also has two much smaller moons, called Nix and Hydra.

FIXED IN THE SKY

Pluto's day is 6.4 Earth days long, the same time that Charon takes to orbit the planet. As a result, Charon never moves across Pluto's sky. From the other side of Pluto, you would never even know Charon was there!

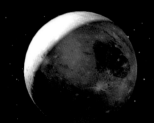

Pluto

Charon

Pluto and Charon have the same face locked toward each other. Being so close and similar in size to Pluto, Charon does not really orbit its neighbor. Instead, the two objects both swing around a point located between them. Sometimes astronomers call Pluto and Charon a double planet.

as it orbits Pluto, the two worlds keep the same side (red dots) facing each other all the time.

Charon

Pluto

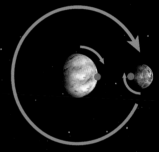

This is a view of Pluto from the surface of the moon Hydra, with Charon in the distance. Nix is a tiny dot far to the left.

STUDYING THE OUTER PLANETS

Uranus, Neptune, and Pluto were all discovered later than the other planets because they are much harder to see.

NEW PLANET

Although Uranus is just visible with the naked eye, no one realized it was a planet until long after the invention of the telescope.

Uranus was discovered accidentally by the British astronomer William Herschel on March 13, 1781. Herschel was making a map of the sky when he saw a fuzzy green dot. When he plotted the object's movement, he found that it was moving slowly. That meant it was a distant planet. At first astronomers called the new planet Herschel. Many years later, everyone agreed to name it Uranus, after the ancient Greek sky god.

William Herschel called the new planet George's Star, in honor of the king of England at the time.

ANYTHING ELSE OUT THERE?

Astronomers were puzzled over the way Uranus moved in its orbit. They suspected the gravity of another more distant planet was pulling on Uranus. Frenchman Urbain Leverrier calculated where this mystery planet was in 1784, and German Johann Gottfried Galle used his calculations to locate Neptune.

FINDING PLANET X

Like Uranus, Neptune had an unexpected orbit. Was there yet another planet even farther beyond? The search began for this planet X.

Pluto was the Roman god of the dead. Charon was the boatman who rowed the dead into the underworld.

Clyde Tombaugh spotted Pluto in photographs taken in 1930 at the Lowell Observatory in Arizona.

In 1930, a young astronomer named Clyde Tombaugh found Pluto by studying photographs of small patches of the sky. By comparing two images of the same area taken a few days apart, Tombaugh could see if anything had moved. By a great stroke of luck, Tombaugh's pictures had a faint, shifting dot in them, 250 times fainter than Neptune. It was named Pluto after the god of the underworld. This kind of search is now done by computer and it located Eris in 2005.

LONELY VISITOR

Most of our knowledge of the outer planets comes from the *Voyager 2* **probe**. This was sent off from Earth in 1977 and traveled to Uranus via Jupiter and Saturn. *Voyager 2* arrived at Uranus in 1986. It flew straight past and had only a few hours to study the planet. The probe took photographs of Uranus's rings and the moon Miranda.

The last stop, Neptune, was reached in 1989. *Voyager 2* flew near Neptune's north pole before sweeping south to fly past Triton.

FIXED IN THE SKY

No space probes have yet visited Pluto. Most ideas about Pluto come from comparisons with Triton, which is thought to have been a **Kuiper Belt** object similar to Pluto until it was captured by Neptune's gravity.

In 2006, the *New Horizons* mission was begun. The probe will fly by Pluto in 2015. Then it will continue on into the Kuiper Belt.

New Horizons will reach Pluto just in time. In 2020, the planet will start its long winter and the air will freeze for 200 years! **. . . . ●**

COULD HUMANS LIVE THERE?

You have been in space for several decades but were asleep for most of it. Would humans ever make the same journey to find a place to live?

FUEL NEEDED

Human settlers near Uranus, Neptune, or Pluto would need to bring a long-term power supply with them. Solar panels are useless this far away from the Sun. However, the outer solar system is rich in the other key requirement for life—water. Water can be split into its chemical components to make oxygen for breathing and hydrogen for rocket fuel.

WHY GO?

There is little reason to settle there. The outer solar system has nothing we cannot get more easily from the inner planets, and exploration is cheaper and safer when it is done by robotic space probes.

Perhaps one day astronauts will explore Uranus's moon Miranda. ⋅ ⋅ ⋅ ⋅ ●

GLOSSARY

asteroids (AS-teh-roydz) Large chunks of rock left over from when the planets formed.

astronomers (uh-STRAH-nuh-merz) Scientists who study planets and other objects in space.

atmosphere (AT-muh-sfeer) The layer of gas trapped around the surface of a planet.

billion (BIL-yun) One thousand millions.

comets (KAH-mits) Large chunks of ice that grow long, glowing tails when near the Sun.

core (KOR) The central part of a planet.

craters (KRAY-turz) Holes made in the ground when space rocks smash into planets or moons. Volcanoes also produce a type of crater.

crust (KRUST) The solid outer surface of a planet or moon.

equator (ih-KWAY-tur) The imaginary line around the center of a planet, moon, or star that is located midway between the poles.

flickering (FLIH-ker-ing) Burning with an unsteady light.

geysers (GY-zerz) Eruptions of boiling liquid or gas from under ground.

gravity (GRA-vih-tee) The force that pulls objects together. The heavier or closer an object is, the stronger its gravity.

helium (HEE-lee-um) A gas found in the Sun and in the giant planets. Helium is the second-most-common element in the universe.

hydrogen (HY-dreh-jen) The simplest, lightest, and most common element in the universe. Hydrogen makes up most of the gas in the Sun and in the giant planets.

ice giants (YS JY-ints) Huge planets made mostly out of slushy ice. Uranus and Neptune are both ice giants.

impact (IM-pakt) When two objects hit each other.

Kuiper Belt (KY-per BELT) A ring of comets and larger icy worlds orbiting beyond Neptune, including the dwarf planets Pluto and Eris.

lava (LAH-vuh) Melted rock that pours onto a planet's or moon's surface.

magnetic field (mag-NEH-tik FEELD) A region of space around a planet, moon, or star where a compass can detect the north pole.

magnetic poles (mag-NEH-tik POHLZ) Points on planets or moons that a compass points directly toward or directly away from. Earth's magnetic poles are near the North Pole and South Pole.

mantle (MAN-tul) The section of a planet between the core and the crust.

mass (MAS) The measure of the amount of matter in an object. Mass is similar to weight, but objects have weight only when they are on a planet or moon.

methane (MEH-thayn) A gas made of carbon and hydrogen. Methane is a type of organic compound. Organic compounds are substances with carbon in them.

mission (MIH-shun) An expedition to visit a certain place in space, such as a planet.

orbits (OR-bits) Movements around heavier, and usually larger, objects caused by the effect of the heavier object's gravity.

oxygen (OK-sih-jen) The invisible gas in Earth's air that living things breathe in.

planetesimals (pla-neh-TEH-suh-mulz) Small, planetlike balls that formed in the early solar system.

pole (POHL) The top or bottom end of the axis of a planet, moon, or star.

pressure (PREH-shur) A measure of how much the gas pushes down on you.

probe (PROHB) A robot spaceship sent to study the solar system.

radar (RAY-dahr) Technology using radio waves to calculate an object's position or shape.

rings (RINGZ) Circles made up of millions of ice or rock particles orbiting together around a planet.

rotates (ROH-tayts) Spins around a central point, or axis.

satellites (SA-tih-lyts) Objects that orbit others. Moons are natural satellites, while most spacecraft are man-made satellites.

solar system (SOH-ler SIS-tem) The planets, asteroids, and comets that orbit the Sun.

suspended animation (suh-SPEND-ed a-nuh-MAY-shun) A very deep sleep like hibernation. It is not yet possible for humans to go into suspended animation.

temperature (TEM-pur-cher) How hot something is.

tidal heating (TY-dul HEET-ing) A process in which the inside of a planet or moon is warmed by the gravity of a neighboring body.

volcanoes (vol-KAY-nohz) Mountains formed from lava that erupts onto the surface from under ground.

INDEX

WEB SITES

Due to the changing nature of Internet links, PowerKids Press has developed an online list of Web sites related to the subject of this book. This site is updated regularly. Please use this link to access the list:
www.powerkidslinks.com/dsol/urannpl/